50 Perfect Portion Dishes

By: Kelly Johnson

Table of Contents

- Mini Meatloaf Muffins
- Single-Serve Mac and Cheese
- Personal Chicken Pot Pie
- Individual Lasagna Cups
- Stuffed Bell Peppers
- Baked Egg Muffins
- Mini Shepherd's Pie
- Single-Serve Quiche
- Zucchini Pizza Boats
- Shrimp and Grits in Ramekins
- Stuffed Portobello Mushrooms
- Baked Oatmeal Cups
- Personal BBQ Chicken Flatbread
- Mini Cheeseburgers
- Mini Chicken Parmesan
- Sweet Potato and Black Bean Bowls
- Single-Serve Tiramisu
- Individual Apple Crisp
- Stuffed Avocado Tuna Salad
- Single-Serve Shakshuka
- Baked Salmon with Veggies in Foil
- Spinach and Feta Stuffed Chicken Breast
- Mini Breakfast Burritos
- Individual Chicken Enchiladas
- Thai Peanut Chicken Lettuce Wraps
- Personal Beef Stroganoff
- Single-Serve Baked Ziti
- Mini Turkey Meatballs
- Personal Caprese Salad Cups
- Greek Yogurt Parfaits
- Individual Chocolate Lava Cakes
- Mini Taco Bowls
- Stuffed Cabbage Rolls
- Crispy Tofu Rice Bowls
- Single-Serve Chicken Alfredo

- Individual French Onion Soup
- Mini Falafel Wraps
- Individual Brownie Skillet
- Baked Pesto Salmon Portions
- Single-Serve Ratatouille
- Mexican Street Corn Cups
- Mini Chicken and Waffles
- Individual Cheesecake Jars
- Spaghetti Squash Boats
- Mini Breakfast Frittatas
- Personal Spinach and Ricotta Stuffed Shells
- Individual Pumpkin Pie Cups
- Greek Chicken Souvlaki Skewers
- Mini Loaded Baked Potatoes
- Personal Shrimp Scampi

Mini Meatloaf Muffins

Ingredients:

- 1 lb ground beef (or turkey)
- ½ cup breadcrumbs
- 1 egg
- ¼ cup ketchup
- 1 teaspoon Worcestershire sauce
- ½ teaspoon garlic powder
- ½ teaspoon onion powder
- Salt and pepper to taste
- ½ cup shredded cheese (optional)

Instructions:

1. **Preheat oven** to 375°F (190°C). Grease a muffin tin.
2. **Mix ingredients:** In a bowl, combine all ingredients.
3. **Fill muffin tin:** Divide mixture evenly into muffin cups.
4. **Bake** for 20-25 minutes until cooked through.
5. **Optional:** Top with extra ketchup or cheese and bake for 5 more minutes.

Single-Serve Mac and Cheese

Ingredients:

- ½ cup elbow macaroni
- ¾ cup milk
- ½ cup shredded cheddar cheese
- ¼ teaspoon garlic powder
- ¼ teaspoon salt
- 1 teaspoon butter

Instructions:

1. **Cook pasta:** Boil macaroni in salted water until tender. Drain.
2. **Melt butter** in a small saucepan, then add milk and cheese. Stir until melted.
3. **Mix pasta:** Add cooked pasta to the cheese sauce and stir.
4. **Serve hot!**

Personal Chicken Pot Pie

Ingredients:

- ½ cup cooked shredded chicken
- ¼ cup frozen mixed vegetables
- ¼ cup chicken broth
- 1 tablespoon heavy cream
- ½ teaspoon cornstarch
- 1 refrigerated biscuit dough

Instructions:

1. **Preheat oven** to 375°F (190°C).
2. **Make filling:** In a pan, heat chicken, vegetables, broth, and cream. Stir in cornstarch to thicken.
3. **Fill ramekin:** Pour mixture into a small baking dish.
4. **Top with biscuit** and bake for 20-25 minutes until golden brown.

Individual Lasagna Cups

Ingredients:

- 4 wonton wrappers
- ½ cup ricotta cheese
- ¼ cup shredded mozzarella
- ¼ cup marinara sauce
- ¼ teaspoon garlic powder
- ¼ teaspoon Italian seasoning

Instructions:

1. **Preheat oven** to 375°F (190°C). Grease a muffin tin.
2. **Layer:** Place a wonton wrapper in each cup, add ricotta, marinara, mozzarella, and seasoning. Repeat layers.
3. **Bake** for 15-20 minutes until bubbly.

Stuffed Bell Peppers

Ingredients:

- 1 bell pepper, halved and seeds removed
- ½ cup cooked ground beef or turkey
- ¼ cup cooked rice
- ¼ cup tomato sauce
- ¼ teaspoon garlic powder
- ¼ teaspoon salt
- ¼ cup shredded cheese

Instructions:

1. **Preheat oven** to 375°F (190°C).
2. **Mix filling:** Combine meat, rice, sauce, and seasoning.
3. **Fill pepper halves:** Stuff the peppers with the mixture.
4. **Bake for 20 minutes,** then top with cheese and bake for 5 more minutes.

Baked Egg Muffins

Ingredients:

- 3 eggs
- ¼ cup diced vegetables (spinach, bell peppers, onions)
- ¼ cup shredded cheese
- ¼ teaspoon salt and pepper

Instructions:

1. **Preheat oven** to 375°F (190°C). Grease a muffin tin.
2. **Whisk eggs** and mix in veggies and cheese.
3. **Pour into muffin cups** and bake for 15-20 minutes until set.

Mini Shepherd's Pie

Ingredients:

- ½ cup ground beef or lamb
- ¼ cup frozen mixed vegetables
- ¼ cup beef broth
- ½ cup mashed potatoes
- ¼ teaspoon garlic powder
- Salt and pepper to taste

Instructions:

1. **Preheat oven** to 375°F (190°C).
2. **Cook meat and veggies:** Brown the meat in a pan, add vegetables, broth, and seasonings.
3. **Assemble:** Spoon meat mixture into a ramekin and top with mashed potatoes.
4. **Bake** for 20 minutes until golden.

Single-Serve Quiche

Ingredients:

- 1 egg
- ¼ cup milk
- ¼ cup shredded cheese
- ¼ cup diced vegetables or ham
- 1 small pie crust (or omit for crustless)

Instructions:

1. **Preheat oven** to 375°F (190°C). Grease a ramekin.
2. **Mix filling:** Beat egg, milk, cheese, and veggies.
3. **Pour into ramekin** and bake for 20-25 minutes until set.

Zucchini Pizza Boats

Ingredients:

- 1 zucchini, halved
- ¼ cup marinara sauce
- ¼ cup shredded mozzarella
- ¼ teaspoon Italian seasoning
- 4 slices pepperoni (optional)

Instructions:

1. **Preheat oven** to 375°F (190°C).
2. **Scoop out some zucchini flesh** to create a boat shape.
3. **Fill with sauce and cheese,** then top with seasoning and pepperoni.
4. **Bake** for 15-20 minutes until cheese melts.

Shrimp and Grits in Ramekins

Ingredients:

- ½ cup cooked shrimp
- ½ cup cooked grits
- ¼ cup shredded cheddar cheese
- ¼ teaspoon garlic powder
- ¼ teaspoon paprika

Instructions:

1. **Preheat oven** to 375°F (190°C).
2. **Mix grits** with cheese and seasonings. Pour into a ramekin.
3. **Top with shrimp** and bake for 10-15 minutes.

Stuffed Portobello Mushrooms

Ingredients:

- 1 large Portobello mushroom
- ¼ cup cooked quinoa (or rice)
- ¼ cup sautéed spinach
- 2 tablespoons feta cheese
- ¼ teaspoon garlic powder
- ¼ teaspoon salt & pepper

Instructions:

1. **Preheat oven** to 375°F (190°C).
2. **Remove mushroom stem** and clean the cap.
3. **Mix filling:** Combine quinoa, spinach, feta, and seasoning.
4. **Stuff the mushroom** and bake for 15-20 minutes until tender.

Baked Oatmeal Cups

Ingredients:

- ½ cup rolled oats
- ½ cup milk (or plant-based alternative)
- 1 tablespoon honey or maple syrup
- ¼ teaspoon cinnamon
- ¼ teaspoon vanilla extract
- ¼ cup berries or nuts

Instructions:

1. **Preheat oven** to 375°F (190°C). Grease a muffin tin.
2. **Mix ingredients** and pour into a muffin cup.
3. **Bake for 20 minutes** until set.

Personal BBQ Chicken Flatbread

Ingredients:

- 1 small naan or flatbread
- ¼ cup cooked shredded chicken
- 2 tablespoons BBQ sauce
- ¼ cup shredded mozzarella cheese
- 1 tablespoon red onion (thinly sliced)
- 1 teaspoon chopped cilantro

Instructions:

1. **Preheat oven** to 400°F (200°C).
2. **Spread BBQ sauce** over the flatbread.
3. **Top with chicken, cheese, and onions.**
4. **Bake for 10 minutes** until crispy. Garnish with cilantro.

Mini Cheeseburgers

Ingredients:

- ¼ lb ground beef
- ½ teaspoon salt
- ¼ teaspoon black pepper
- ¼ teaspoon garlic powder
- 1 small slider bun
- 1 slice cheese
- 1 slice tomato & lettuce

Instructions:

1. **Preheat skillet** over medium heat.
2. **Form beef into a small patty,** season with salt, pepper, and garlic powder.
3. **Cook for 3-4 minutes per side.**
4. **Melt cheese on top** and assemble with bun and toppings.

Mini Chicken Parmesan

Ingredients:

- 1 small chicken breast
- ¼ cup marinara sauce
- ¼ cup shredded mozzarella
- ¼ teaspoon Italian seasoning
- 1 tablespoon grated Parmesan
- 1 small egg
- ¼ cup breadcrumbs

Instructions:

1. **Preheat oven** to 375°F (190°C).
2. **Dip chicken** in egg, then coat with breadcrumbs.
3. **Bake for 15 minutes.**
4. **Top with marinara & cheese,** then bake for 5 more minutes.

Sweet Potato and Black Bean Bowls

Ingredients:

- ½ cup roasted sweet potatoes
- ¼ cup black beans
- ¼ cup cooked quinoa or rice
- 1 tablespoon avocado
- ¼ teaspoon cumin
- 1 tablespoon Greek yogurt (optional)

Instructions:

1. **Roast sweet potatoes** at 400°F (200°C) for 20 minutes.
2. **Assemble bowl** with black beans, quinoa, avocado, and seasoning.
3. **Top with Greek yogurt** if desired.

Single-Serve Tiramisu

Ingredients:

- 2 ladyfinger biscuits
- ¼ cup brewed coffee (cooled)
- ¼ cup mascarpone cheese
- 1 tablespoon sugar
- ¼ teaspoon vanilla extract
- 1 tablespoon cocoa powder

Instructions:

1. **Mix mascarpone, sugar, and vanilla.**
2. **Dip ladyfingers** in coffee and layer with mascarpone mixture.
3. **Repeat layers and dust with cocoa powder.**
4. **Refrigerate for 1 hour before serving.**

Individual Apple Crisp

Ingredients:

- 1 small apple, diced
- 1 tablespoon brown sugar
- ¼ teaspoon cinnamon
- ¼ cup oats
- 1 tablespoon butter

Instructions:

1. **Preheat oven** to 375°F (190°C).
2. **Toss apples** with sugar and cinnamon.
3. **Mix oats & butter** and sprinkle on top.
4. **Bake for 20 minutes** until golden brown.

Stuffed Avocado Tuna Salad

Ingredients:

- 1 ripe avocado, halved
- ¼ cup canned tuna
- 1 tablespoon Greek yogurt or mayo
- ¼ teaspoon lemon juice
- Salt & pepper to taste

Instructions:

1. **Mix tuna with yogurt, lemon, salt, and pepper.**
2. **Scoop out some avocado flesh** and mix with tuna.
3. **Fill avocado halves** and serve.

Single-Serve Shakshuka

Ingredients:

- ½ cup crushed tomatoes
- 1 egg
- ¼ teaspoon cumin
- ¼ teaspoon paprika
- 1 tablespoon feta cheese

Instructions:

1. **Heat tomatoes in a small skillet.**
2. **Add seasonings** and simmer for 5 minutes.
3. **Crack egg into sauce** and cook until set.
4. **Top with feta and serve.**

Baked Salmon with Veggies in Foil

Ingredients:

- 1 salmon fillet
- ¼ cup zucchini & bell pepper slices
- 1 tablespoon olive oil
- ¼ teaspoon garlic powder
- Salt & pepper to taste

Instructions:

1. **Preheat oven** to 375°F (190°C).
2. **Place salmon on foil,** top with veggies & seasonings.
3. **Wrap tightly and bake for 15 minutes.**

Spinach and Feta Stuffed Chicken Breast

Ingredients:

- 1 small chicken breast
- ¼ cup fresh spinach, chopped
- 2 tablespoons feta cheese
- ¼ teaspoon garlic powder
- ¼ teaspoon black pepper
- 1 teaspoon olive oil

Instructions:

1. **Preheat oven** to 375°F (190°C).
2. **Slice chicken breast** to create a pocket.
3. **Mix spinach, feta, garlic powder, and pepper.** Stuff into the chicken.
4. **Secure with toothpicks, brush with olive oil,** and bake for 20-25 minutes.

Mini Breakfast Burritos

Ingredients:

- 1 small tortilla
- 1 egg, scrambled
- 1 tablespoon shredded cheese
- 1 tablespoon cooked sausage or beans
- 1 tablespoon salsa

Instructions:

1. **Scramble egg** and cook sausage (if using).
2. **Fill tortilla** with egg, cheese, sausage, and salsa.
3. **Roll and heat in a pan** for 1-2 minutes until crispy.

Individual Chicken Enchiladas

Ingredients:

- 1 small tortilla
- ¼ cup shredded cooked chicken
- 2 tablespoons enchilada sauce
- 2 tablespoons shredded cheese
- 1 tablespoon chopped cilantro

Instructions:

1. **Preheat oven** to 375°F (190°C).
2. **Fill tortilla** with chicken and 1 tablespoon sauce, then roll it.
3. **Place in a small baking dish,** top with sauce and cheese.
4. **Bake for 10-12 minutes.** Garnish with cilantro.

Thai Peanut Chicken Lettuce Wraps

Ingredients:

- 1 cooked chicken breast, shredded
- 1 tablespoon peanut butter
- 1 teaspoon soy sauce
- ½ teaspoon lime juice
- 2 large lettuce leaves

Instructions:

1. **Mix chicken with peanut butter, soy sauce, and lime juice.**
2. **Spoon into lettuce leaves** and serve.

Personal Beef Stroganoff

Ingredients:

- ¼ cup cooked beef strips
- ¼ cup mushrooms, sliced
- 2 tablespoons sour cream
- ¼ cup cooked egg noodles
- ½ teaspoon Worcestershire sauce

Instructions:

1. **Sauté mushrooms** in a pan over medium heat.
2. **Add beef, Worcestershire sauce, and sour cream.** Stir to combine.
3. **Serve over cooked egg noodles.**

Single-Serve Baked Ziti

Ingredients:

- ½ cup cooked ziti pasta
- ¼ cup marinara sauce
- 2 tablespoons ricotta cheese
- 2 tablespoons shredded mozzarella

Instructions:

1. **Preheat oven** to 375°F (190°C).
2. **Mix pasta with marinara and ricotta.**
3. **Transfer to a small baking dish,** top with mozzarella.
4. **Bake for 10-12 minutes** until cheese is melted.

Mini Turkey Meatballs

Ingredients:

- ¼ lb ground turkey
- 2 tablespoons breadcrumbs
- ½ teaspoon garlic powder
- ½ teaspoon Italian seasoning
- 1 teaspoon olive oil

Instructions:

1. **Preheat oven** to 375°F (190°C).
2. **Mix turkey with breadcrumbs and seasonings.** Form small meatballs.
3. **Place on a baking sheet,** drizzle with olive oil.
4. **Bake for 15-18 minutes** until golden brown.

Personal Caprese Salad Cups

Ingredients:

- 5 cherry tomatoes, halved
- ¼ cup fresh mozzarella, cubed
- 1 tablespoon fresh basil, chopped
- 1 teaspoon balsamic glaze

Instructions:

1. **Combine tomatoes, mozzarella, and basil** in a small cup.
2. **Drizzle with balsamic glaze.**

Greek Yogurt Parfaits

Ingredients:

- ½ cup Greek yogurt
- 2 tablespoons granola
- 2 tablespoons mixed berries
- 1 teaspoon honey

Instructions:

1. **Layer yogurt, berries, and granola** in a cup.
2. **Drizzle with honey** before serving.

Individual Chocolate Lava Cake

Ingredients:

- 2 tablespoons butter
- ¼ cup dark chocolate, chopped
- ¼ cup powdered sugar
- 1 egg
- 2 tablespoons flour

Instructions:

1. **Preheat oven** to 400°F (200°C). Grease a small ramekin.
2. **Melt butter and chocolate** together. Stir in sugar, egg, and flour.
3. **Pour batter into the ramekin** and bake for 10-12 minutes.
4. **Serve warm** for a gooey center.

Mini Taco Bowls

Ingredients:

- 1 small tortilla
- ¼ cup ground beef or turkey
- 1 tablespoon taco seasoning
- 2 tablespoons shredded cheese
- 1 tablespoon salsa
- 1 tablespoon sour cream
- 1 tablespoon chopped lettuce

Instructions:

1. **Preheat oven** to 375°F (190°C). Press the tortilla into a small oven-safe bowl or muffin tin.
2. **Bake for 8-10 minutes** until crisp.
3. **Cook ground meat** with taco seasoning.
4. **Fill tortilla shell** with cooked meat, cheese, salsa, lettuce, and sour cream.

Stuffed Cabbage Rolls

Ingredients:

- 1 large cabbage leaf
- ¼ cup ground beef or turkey
- 2 tablespoons cooked rice
- 1 tablespoon tomato sauce
- ½ teaspoon garlic powder

Instructions:

1. **Boil cabbage leaf** for 1-2 minutes to soften.
2. **Mix meat, rice, garlic powder, and tomato sauce.**
3. **Place filling in cabbage leaf, roll tightly,** and secure with a toothpick.
4. **Bake in a small dish with extra tomato sauce at 375°F (190°C) for 20 minutes.**

Crispy Tofu Rice Bowls

Ingredients:

- ¼ block firm tofu, cubed
- ½ cup cooked rice
- 1 teaspoon soy sauce
- 1 teaspoon sesame oil
- ¼ cup mixed vegetables
- ½ teaspoon garlic powder

Instructions:

1. **Pat tofu dry** and season with garlic powder.
2. **Pan-fry in sesame oil** until golden brown.
3. **Assemble bowl** with rice, vegetables, tofu, and soy sauce drizzle.

Single-Serve Chicken Alfredo

Ingredients:

- ½ cup cooked pasta
- ¼ cup cooked chicken, sliced
- 2 tablespoons Alfredo sauce
- 1 tablespoon Parmesan cheese

Instructions:

1. **Warm Alfredo sauce** in a small pan.
2. **Add cooked pasta and chicken,** stirring to coat.
3. **Top with Parmesan and serve hot.**

Individual French Onion Soup

Ingredients:

- ½ onion, thinly sliced
- 1 cup beef broth
- 1 small slice of baguette
- 2 tablespoons shredded Gruyère cheese
- ½ teaspoon thyme

Instructions:

1. **Sauté onions** in a small pot until caramelized.
2. **Add broth and thyme, simmer** for 10 minutes.
3. **Pour into an oven-safe bowl,** top with baguette and cheese.
4. **Broil until cheese is melted.**

Mini Falafel Wraps

Ingredients:

- 2 small falafel balls
- 1 small pita or tortilla
- 1 tablespoon hummus
- 1 tablespoon chopped cucumber
- 1 tablespoon yogurt sauce

Instructions:

1. **Warm falafel and pita.**
2. **Spread hummus on pita,** add falafel, cucumber, and yogurt sauce.
3. **Wrap and enjoy!**

Individual Brownie Skillet

Ingredients:

- 2 tablespoons butter
- ¼ cup dark chocolate, chopped
- ¼ cup sugar
- 1 egg
- 3 tablespoons flour

Instructions:

1. **Preheat oven** to 350°F (175°C).
2. **Melt butter and chocolate together.**
3. **Stir in sugar, egg, and flour.**
4. **Bake in a small skillet for 10-12 minutes.**

Baked Pesto Salmon Portions

Ingredients:

- 1 small salmon fillet
- 1 tablespoon pesto
- ½ teaspoon lemon juice

Instructions:

1. **Preheat oven** to 375°F (190°C).
2. **Spread pesto** over salmon.
3. **Bake for 12-15 minutes** until flaky.
4. **Drizzle with lemon juice before serving.**

Single-Serve Ratatouille

Ingredients:

- ¼ cup diced zucchini
- ¼ cup diced eggplant
- ¼ cup diced bell pepper
- ¼ cup tomato sauce
- ½ teaspoon garlic powder
- ½ teaspoon olive oil

Instructions:

1. **Sauté vegetables** in olive oil until tender.
2. **Add tomato sauce and garlic powder,** simmer for 5 minutes.
3. **Serve hot.**

Mexican Street Corn Cups

Ingredients:

- ½ cup corn (cooked)
- 1 tablespoon mayonnaise
- 1 tablespoon crumbled cotija cheese
- ½ teaspoon chili powder
- ½ teaspoon lime juice

Instructions:

1. **Mix all ingredients in a cup.**
2. **Stir well and enjoy!**

Mini Chicken and Waffles

Ingredients:

- 2 mini waffles
- 1 small fried chicken tender
- 1 tablespoon maple syrup
- ½ teaspoon hot sauce (optional)

Instructions:

1. **Toast waffles** until golden brown.
2. **Place chicken tender** between waffles.
3. **Drizzle with maple syrup** and optional hot sauce.

Individual Cheesecake Jars

Ingredients:

- ¼ cup crushed graham crackers
- 2 tablespoons cream cheese, softened
- 1 tablespoon sugar
- 1 tablespoon Greek yogurt
- ¼ teaspoon vanilla extract
- 2 tablespoons fruit compote or jam

Instructions:

1. **Mix cream cheese, sugar, yogurt, and vanilla.**
2. **Layer graham cracker crumbs, cream cheese mixture, and fruit in a small jar.**
3. **Chill for 30 minutes before serving.**

Spaghetti Squash Boats

Ingredients:

- ½ small spaghetti squash
- ¼ cup marinara sauce
- ¼ cup cooked ground turkey or beef
- 1 tablespoon Parmesan cheese

Instructions:

1. **Roast spaghetti squash at 375°F (190°C) for 25 minutes.**
2. **Scrape strands with a fork.**
3. **Mix with marinara and meat, then place back in the shell.**
4. **Top with Parmesan and bake for 5 more minutes.**

Mini Breakfast Frittatas

Ingredients:

- 1 egg
- 1 tablespoon milk
- 1 tablespoon shredded cheese
- 2 tablespoons diced vegetables (spinach, peppers, or mushrooms)

Instructions:

1. **Whisk egg and milk, then mix in vegetables and cheese.**
2. **Pour into a greased muffin tin.**
3. **Bake at 375°F (190°C) for 12-15 minutes.**

Personal Spinach and Ricotta Stuffed Shells

Ingredients:

- 3 jumbo pasta shells, cooked
- 2 tablespoons ricotta cheese
- 1 tablespoon cooked spinach, chopped
- ¼ teaspoon garlic powder
- ¼ cup marinara sauce
- 1 tablespoon shredded mozzarella

Instructions:

1. **Mix ricotta, spinach, and garlic powder.**
2. **Stuff into pasta shells.**
3. **Place in a small dish with marinara sauce.**
4. **Top with mozzarella and bake at 375°F (190°C) for 15 minutes.**

Individual Pumpkin Pie Cups

Ingredients:

- ¼ cup pumpkin puree
- 1 tablespoon brown sugar
- ¼ teaspoon pumpkin spice
- 1 tablespoon heavy cream
- 1 small graham cracker, crushed

Instructions:

1. **Mix pumpkin, sugar, spice, and cream.**
2. **Layer with crushed graham cracker in a small cup.**
3. **Chill before serving.**

Greek Chicken Souvlaki Skewers

Ingredients:

- 3 small chicken cubes
- ½ teaspoon olive oil
- ½ teaspoon lemon juice
- ¼ teaspoon oregano
- ¼ teaspoon garlic powder
- 1 small wooden skewer

Instructions:

1. **Marinate chicken** in olive oil, lemon juice, and spices for 15 minutes.
2. **Thread onto skewer** and grill or pan-cook until done.

Mini Loaded Baked Potatoes

Ingredients:

- 1 small baked potato
- 1 tablespoon sour cream
- 1 tablespoon shredded cheddar cheese
- ½ tablespoon cooked bacon bits
- ½ teaspoon chopped chives

Instructions:

1. **Bake potato at 375°F (190°C) until tender.**
2. **Cut open and top with cheese, bacon, sour cream, and chives.**

Personal Shrimp Scampi

Ingredients:

- 4 shrimp, peeled and deveined
- ½ tablespoon butter
- ½ teaspoon minced garlic
- ¼ cup cooked spaghetti
- ½ tablespoon lemon juice
- 1 teaspoon chopped parsley

Instructions:

1. **Sauté shrimp in butter and garlic** until pink.
2. **Toss with spaghetti and lemon juice.**
3. **Garnish with parsley and serve hot.**

www.ingramcontent.com/pod-product-compliance
Lightning Source LLC
LaVergne TN
LVHW061955070526
838199LV00060B/4142